RAILWAY
• HALSGROVE •
SERIES

LAST DAYS OF STEAM
ON THE MIDLAND REGION

ROGER MALONE

HALSGROVE

First published in Great Britain in 2010

British Library Cataloguing-in-Publication Data
A CIP record for this title is available from the British Library

ISBN 978 1 84114 992 9

HALSGROVE
Halsgrove House,
Ryelands Industrial Estate,
Bagley Road, Wellington, Somerset TA21 9PZ
Tel: 01823 653777   Fax: 01823 216796
email: sales@halsgrove.com

Part of the Halsgrove group of companies.
Information on all Halsgrove titles is available at: www.halsgrove.com

Printed and bound in China by Toppan Leefung Printing Ltd

Introduction

THE END. It arrived with a celebration of what remained – and lament for what was almost over.

To some, steam's demise in 1968 was merely a belated step towards progress via total dieselisation. But to the steam enthusiast, nurtured on the sulphurous breath of these iron steeds, this last goodbye was anathema.

For years life had altered little, even in the wake of Nationalisation when, in 1948, the Big Four (SR, LMS, GWR and LNER) became British Railways. Liveries changed, the old company logos disappeared and were replaced with BR's all embracing 'lion and wheel' emblem; standard classes, designed for easier maintenance, were added to the now amalgamated locomotive fleet; but steam was still king and the old order seemed eternal. Rural branch lines threaded the countryside cocooned in rustic time warps; and all the infrastructure, the platform paraphernalia and lineside furniture that supported the system, seemed reassuringly constant.

But ultimately that was an illusion shattered by the mid-sixties. The writing had been on the wall for a while, although initially few enthusiasts read it; and those that did found it hard to credit their beloved status quo was in modernisation meltdown. Swiftly, what was once part of the everyday scene – turntables, semaphore signals, water towers, country stations – was vanishing.

To those hitherto not alert to the changing face of the railway network here was a resounding alarm bell. An eleventh hour clarion call, it galvanised into action many enthusiasts determined to make the most of what was left.

With a quickening pace steam-hauled roots were axed across the system, and locomotives ignominiously withdrawn for scrap. Some were cut up straight away. For others good fortune saw them ferried to the famous Woodham Brothers scrapyard in Barry, South Wales. Here, after lingering in this locomotive graveyard, many were rescued and restored to pristine condition by dedicated preservationists.

Throughout the mid-sixties, the steam cull was relentless. The Western Region carried it out with almost indecent haste, while the Southern Region held on to 1967 along with the North East. The Midland Region was the last to go. It had suffered serious steam casualties as depot after depot closed, yet incredibly a pocket of three Lancashire sheds survived to the last. The trio, Carnforth, Lostock Hall (near Preston) and Rose Grove (near Burnley) achieved almost celebrity status in 1968 as the only steam motive power depots still operating in the whole country.

Steam had become entrenched here, braced for one valiant last stand. These hallowed locations duly became a Mecca for every enthusiast able to make the pilgrimage. In reality, there was a time, with richer pickings to be found elsewhere, they would not have enjoyed such fame. But in the final loco shed lottery the dice had rolled and, against all odds and on borrowed time, they were winners.

Time ticked towards an almost surreal extinction, with a countdown cold as the steel of a locomotive whose fire had been dropped for the last time. Out of the final year arrived the final month, final week and, ultimately, the final day: August 4, 1968. On that day the three depots' collective demise signalled the last breath of British Railways' working steam. It seemed hardly credible that a mode of transport with us since George Stephenson built the world's first public railways – the Stockton and Darlington Railway in 1825 and Liverpool-Manchester Railway in 1830 – would abruptly end on such an ordinary sunny summer Sunday. But it had. It was over.

I consider myself fortunate to have been there at the end. At seventeen, I had – taking into account the pressures of school, pocket money and the understandable limitations of parential goodwill – been capturing what I could of steam on camera since 1965. August 4 was a poignant closure on an enthusiasm that had, prompted I think by that first childhood train set, evolved into a passion.

During the previous two years, on what was more akin to home turf, I witnessed a fair proportion of steam's Indian summer on the Southern Region. Miraculously, I convinced the family it would be great if the annual camping holiday coincided with that momentous week in the North West when working steam blithely plodded about its mundane business before being abruptly consigned to history.

For me that time provided an unforgettable ringside seat to this last curtain call. Here, amidst rusty sidings, neglected infrastructure and embankments flushed pink with swathes of rose-bay-willowherb, those lingering locomotives were to breath their last. Hulks of mere metal they may be to non-sentimentalists, but many an enthusiast could not help but anthropomorphise them into something almost living and, consequently, something dying.

Railway photography for me began three years previously when I took my first railway images armed with a 35mm camera loaded with transparency film. At fourteen, I had got the bug for transparencies after a slide show by a friend of my father left me spell-bound. Another good piece of fortune, which allowed steam to loiter where it would otherwise be bereft, was boundary changes within the British Railways network.

So a Welsh holiday benefited from the still steam-friendly Midland Region taking over some Western Region territories. This prolonged steam on the former Cambrian route out of Shrewsbury to Aberystwyth and Pwllheli – formerly a traditional Great Western stomping ground. The mainstay of latter-day Western Region steam motive power, the attractively-proportioned Manors, had been replaced by the more utilitarian BR Standard Class 4 4-6-0s. Less glamorous to the purists maybe, but I was more than delighted to have a brief encounter with them.

My first British Railways steam locomotive framed in the viewfinder was Standard Class 4 No 75013 departing from Towyn with an up freight on 25 July 1965. For a new recruit to such subject matter it was a memorable moment. We had travelled up to the Talyllyn Railway from West Wales for a trip on the 1ft 11ins narrow gauge track out to Abergynolwyn and back. The Towyn terminus of this narrow gauge railway was in close proximity to the Cambrian mainline. Walking back to the car there was No 75013 fortuitously pulling away from the station.

During that holiday a visit was made to the Vale of Rheidol Railway, British Railway's only narrow gauge railway. Its three locomotives, 'Owain Glyndwr', 'Llywelyn' and 'Prince of Wales', were destined to become the only steam locomotives operated by British Railways after the end of steam. Bizarrely, they would also be the only steam engines ever to appear in BR corporate blue sporting the new double arrow logo. This brave new livery was to flag up the modern image, so seemed especially incongruous on a class of locomotive introduced in 1902.

Holidaying on the Lleyn Peninsula the following year meant the chance to visit the Cambrian once more, and also get a glimpse of the North Wales main line to Holyhead. Like any railway-obsessed teenager lacking independent means I relied on much goodwill for facilitating the occasional railway detour.

Getting a picture was often a question of being in the right place at the right time and keeping a sharp eye out when close to a railway line! That certainly was the case when I photographed BR Standard Class 4 No 75055 hauling the Cambrian Coast Express into Barmouth with the impressive slopes of Cadair Idris brooding in the background. On another occasion, while at Criccieth, it was a matter of stringing out time by a level crossing in the hope of seeing an up-freight train pass that I had earlier noticed being marshalled at Pwllheli. Fortunately, it put in an appearance in the shape of green-liveried BR Standard Class 4 4-6-0 No 75007.

Holyhead and Llandudno Junction provided two excellent outings. In the depths of Holyhead shed I saw my fist BR Britannia Class Pacific 'Venus'. At Llandudno Junction, apart from stepping into one of the cleanest sheds I have ever seen, there was the splendid sight of a 'Jinty' 0-6-0T on shunting duty. A once ubiquitous ex-LMS tank engine, it was nevertheless a great coup for me.

While the last day of steam is indelibly inscribed on my consciousness, another railway date that resonates like August 4, 1968, but for less oppressive reasons is March 4, 1966.

This was the last weekend of through trains from Paddington to Birkenhead; the final steam-hauled Cambrian Coast Express to Aberystwyth, and the finale of steam out of Shrewsbury. It also spelt the end of the last stretch of track in the British Isles where steam traction was timed at over 60mph start to stop. In the early months of 1967, the Chester and Shrewsbury enginemen put in many fine performances between Gobowen and Shrewsbury, with speeds reaching over 90mph. To mark the occasion Ian Allan ran two specials hauled by GWR pedigrees 'Clun Castle' and 'Pendennis Castle'.

A school friend and I decided to travel from Plymouth to Shrewsbury, and then catch a steam-hauled service to Chester and return. It was one of those great days of fun, high spirits and an abundance of steam.

By the time we arrived, Shrewsbury Station was awash with enthusiasts. When the first of the Ian Allan specials arrived behind GWR 4-6-0 No 7029 'Clun Castle', disembarking enthusiasts surged to the platform ends like fans mobbing a film star. The atmosphere was electric. Photographers even shinned up signals for better vantage points. After taking water, 'Clun Castle' made a sure-footed, calculatingly-showy departure worthy of such attention.

The train we boarded for Chester was hauled by 'Black Five' 4-6-0 No 45042, and was sandwiched between the path of the two Castle Class locomotives. Hanging out of a window in the first coach we watched the 'Black Five' all the way. The crew delivered an exhilarating performance. The tender swayed back and forth with an occasionally disconcerting counter lurch to our coach as the locomotive bowled along, driver and fireman determined to notch up a spirited run on this final weekend.

I felt the part with a pair of goggles borrowed from my father. I'd previously noted ardent enthusiasts hanging out windows doing their earth-bound impression of Biggles. To an impressionable youth the look suggested a style statement of the enthusiast cognoscente, with the advantage, when hanging out carriage windows, of avoiding smuts in the eye. I have often joked that a smut in the eye is part of the pleasure of pursuing steam. Fine words until you get one – then you feel less privileged. My friend, meanwhile, felt pretty natty in a hat until it was dislodged mid-journey by the Black Five's slipstream to gales of shared laughter. En route we passed a 'Black Five', a couple of 8Fs and the only Crosti-boilered Class 9F 2-10-0 in business, No 92026.

Our return trip, behind BR Standard Class 5 4-6-0 No 73093, was less entertaining as the train was so packed with enthusiasts it was impossible to commandeer a window.

Shrewsbury Station was still busy with steam. As we headed back to Plymouth I saw a couple of LMS Class 4 2-6-0s sidelined, and a grimy Stanier 8F taking water on Shrewsbury shed, which closed at the end of the weekend. It was late afternoon and the weakening sunlight, mingling with steam, created a poignant aura. It was a fitting last image as we settled down for the long journey home.

More encounters with Midland steam followed in 1967, including camping by the side of Shap, the famous gradient on the West Coast Main Line, midway between Crewe and Carlisle. Here, a procession of trains passed in a rapturous crescendo of pounding exhaust beats, while my camera chose this iconic location to give up the ghost. Fortunately, my scribbled railway notes salvaged something of those faraway events. Despite more serious issues that leave an indelible mark through life's course, the loss of those images still smarts!

In 1968, and armed with a new camera, steam's eleventh hour beckoned. There were special moments on this last steam pilgrimage, the most memorable being the most emotional. Who could not feel a lump in the throat at the platform atmosphere as the last steam train for Blackpool prepared to depart from Preston?

Adding more weight to the poignancy of the last week was the sight of ex-LMS Class 8F No 48666 straddling the tracks at Rose Grove shed. Mere days from its demise, the locomotive had derailed. Trapped, like some snared creature, rescue came from a breakdown team, but its release would be short lived. It was considered not worth the trouble of repairing any damage caused by the incident, so the locomotive was ignominiously withdrawn from service.

August 4 was a perfect sunny day and, apart from the fact we knew different, it still seemed steam could go on for ever. But late in the afternoon the last surviving Britannia Class Pacific, 'Oliver Cromwell', arrived on shed at Lostock Hall after completing its part in an enthusiasts' special. The polished lines of this simmering giant glinted magnificently in the sun. This was my last image on the last day of steam. It was over.

There would be British Railways' famous £15 Guinea Special a week later on August 11, and, unknown at the time, steam would venture back on the mainline in years to come, with preserved locomotives polished to perfection. But whatever the future held, an era ended here on August 4, 1968.

For a while, like many enthusiasts, I turned my back on the now steamless railway system. But gradually a love of photography drew me back. To everyone's delight British Rail gave permission for occasional steam specials on the main line. Today, more than four decades after working steam's demise, preserved steam continues to re-enact past glories. Specials, hauled by celebrated locomotives, power trains packed with enthusiasts on head-turning journeys of nostalgia.

I have ended this book with a visit to the Vale of Rheidol Railway in 1978 with stock in blue livery before BR sold the line, a week in 1987 with the Cardigan Bay Express on the former Cambrian stomping ground, and a selection of some of my favourite images of preserved steam on the main line. The sport of chasing a train and hopefully capturing something of the power and glory of steam is a very seductive one. It is a different world to the sixties when pocket money dictated one film had to be eked out over a number of subjects. Now one subject becomes the target of numerous images.

Much of the detail relating to the images of working BR steam in those last evocative years comes from a diary I wrote at the time. I apologise if any inaccuracies have inadvertently crept in via the pen of a teenage scribe.

THE END OF STEAM

THE CAMBRIAN

BR Standard Class 4 4-6-0 No 75013 eases away from Towyn with an up train bound for Machynlleth. (23 July 1965)

Minus its smokebox number plate, BR Standard Class 4 No 75055 heads the up Cambrian
Coast Express into Barmouth. The impressive Cadair Idris rises majestically in the background. (29 July 1966)

Whistling loudly as it approaches, BR Standard Class 4 No 75009 heads the four-coach Pwllheli-bound section of the Cambrian Coast Express. It is seen skirting a stretch of beach at Tremadog Bay as it approaches Criccieth. (2 August 1966)

BR Standard Class 4 4-6-0 No 75013 approaches Pwllheli Motive Power Depot tender first and hauling a brake van. Along with the steam engines that hauled them, such trucks are a long-gone part of the railway scene. (24 July 1966)

I had noticed BR Standard Class 4 No 75002 building a freight train at Pwllheli in the morning.
Now, around midday, the locomotive, in Swindon Green livery, is seen passing through a level crossing at Criccieth. (5 August 1966)

A visit to Llandudno Junction was rewarded with the sight of ex-LMS 'Jinty' 0-6-0T No 47673
shunting an interesting assortment of wagons. (1 August 1966)

Simmering outside Llandudno Junction Motive Power Depot is a study in Class 5 power. BR Standard Class 5 4-6-0 No 73039 keeps company with a brace of ex-LMS 'Black Fives'. The shed area was host to some fifteen steam locomotives and only one diesel. With the exception of several Standard Class 5s, the locomotives were all Black Fives. (1 August 1966)

Inside Llandudno Junction Motive Power Depot dappled light falls across ex-LMS 'Black Fives' No 45247 and No 44971. (1 August 1966)

Food and drink! An unidentified 'Black Five' is being coaled and watered at Llandudno Junction, in preparation for its next turn of duty. (1 August 1966)

Patience was rewarded at Holyhead when, after a long wait and several diesel departures, BR Standard Class 5 4-6-0 No 73073 backed on to a rake of coaches. A spirited departure ensued, with the rasp of its exhaust resounding off the surrounding buildings. A sign of the times was a hand-painted number filling in for the removed smokebox number plate. Note the 9H shed plate, which implied the locomotive's home shed at the time was Patricroft, and also the different types of headlamps. (4 August 1966)

An ex-LMS 'Black Five' rests at the neck of Holyhead Motive Power Depot in the company of an assortment of trucks. The shed area held nearly a dozen steam locomotives. They were all Black Fives, with the exception of Britannia Class Pacific No 70023 'Venus' which was tucked inside the shed. (4 August 1966)

On the left of the signal box is the mainline approaching the terminus, and, on the right, Holyhead motive power depot packed with power. 'Black Five' No 44683 is steamed up and ready for the next call of duty. (4 August 1966)

SHREWSBURY to CHESTER

'...Our train arrived. The 14.35 Shrewsbury-Chester. This was hauled by a 'Brush' type diesel in the new BR livery. The diesel uncoupled and was replaced, to our delight, by an ex-LMS 'Black Five' 4-6-0 No 45042. As the two Castle specials were running within half an hour of each other, our train was in the middle, with 'Clun Castle' about 15 minutes in front and 'Pendennis Castle' about the same time behind.

After a brief wait, we moved out of the station, running about ten minutes late. As our train passed a goods yard we saw 8F Class 2-8-0 No 48063 with a goods train halted beside a water tower.

This route was the last place where steam still did 'a mile a minute'. When our train stopped at Gobowen I took a picture of the loco, No 45042. Hardly any diesels were to be seen, and all the trains which passed seemed to be hauled by steam. As the train neared Chester, we were joined by the Holyhead lines in a maize of track. A 'Peak' diesel was easing its way in. Our train took a middle track and slowly gained on the diesel until we entered a long tunnel and a steep rock cutting where our train drew to a halt owing to signals. A few minutes later, the Llandudno train emerged from the tunnel and was given right of way, leaving our train behind. We then received right of way and took the south side of a large triangle. Lines that led to the crown of the triangle went northward to Birkenhead. The third side came down to join the main line to Shrewsbury and the North Wales coast.

At the station, two Standard Class 5s waited to take the specials on the last leg of their journey to Birkenhead. After 20 minutes, Castle Class No 4079 'Pendennis Castle' quietly slipped into the station with the second part of the special. Now it was our time to leave. Once more we had steam. No 73093, BR Standard Class 5 was our engine. We left on time, and as we passed the bottom of the triangle I noticed an 8F with several trucks shunting at the Birkenhead end.

The return journey was not as comfortable as it could have been as the train was packed with enthusiasts, so much so that it was nearly impossible to pass along the corridor. (The train from Shrewsbury must have been just as full, but being in an open coach at the very top, next to the locomotive, it was not so noticeable). We passed just as many steam engines going back, but it was impossible to read their numbers. At Shrewsbury a 'Black Five' followed shortly with a train from Chester, and a Standard headed towards Chester with coaching stock, a large number which were in the new corporate blue and silver livery.

Our train was next to arrive, the through Crewe-Plymouth. Hauled by a 'Brush', we now caught our last glimpse of steam passing Shrewsbury Motive Power Depot as we began our long journey home through a land where steam is dead and diesels hold full power.

This weekend was the last for steam traction between Shrewsbury and Chester, the last weekend of the Cambrian Coast Express – which had remained faithful to steam from Shrewsbury to Pwllheli until the end, and also the last weekend of through Paddington-Birkenhead services.

As we sped on from Newport and under the Severn Tunnel, the sights we had seen went pleasantly through our minds as our train raced westwards...'

Diary Extract (4 March 1967)

It pays to keep your camera at the ready. And here, as a keen enthusiast, I reaped my reward at Bristol. The Blue Pullman — a Monday to Friday service to the City — was spending the weekend in the carriage sidings and provided a lucky shot in the early morning sun. (4 March 1967)

The march of the new order is apparent as 'Brush'-type diesel No D1918 eases its train of fuel tanks south through Shrewsbury Station. (4 March 1967)

People who don't love steam engines could not begin to imagine the passion that drove enthusiasts to the platform edges of Shrewsbury Station to pay homage to locomotives that had achieved celebrity status. Here, The Zulu, the first of two specials to mark the end of through workings from Paddington to Birkenhead, arrives behind GWR Castle Class 4-6-0 No 7029 'Clun Castle'. Following in its wake was sister locomotive 'Pendennis Castle'. (4 March 1967)

Having swiftly taken on water 'Clun Castle' was ready to resume its journey to Chester. It departed with a brief bout of wheel slipping, and a barrage of cameras recording its progress. (4 March 1967)

Having reached Chester, 'Clun Castle' is seen turning on the triangle of track to the east of the station where lines part for Birkenhead, Holyhead and Shrewsbury. (4 March 1967)

Hauling the second Ian Allan Special, 'Pendennis Castle' arrives at Chester. (4 March 1967)

*We head for Chester behind 'Black Five' No 45042. Just outside Shrewsbury
it passes 8F Class 2-8-0 No 48063 on a freight train. (4 March 1967)*

A meeting of 'Black Fives'. Heading north No 45042 is about to pass an unidentified member of the class travelling in the opposite direction. (4 March 1967)

*Steam exudes from Crosti-boilered 9F Class 2-10-0 No 92026, as it waits in
a goods loop to allow a faster train to pass before continuing its journey south. (4 March 1967)*

The driver of 'Black Five' No 45042 and his charge take a breather as our train makes a stop at Gobowen. The level crossing at the up end of the station is open to road traffic, and the red 'home' and yellow 'distant' semaphore signals are in the stop position. (4 March 1967)

More steam en route to Chester as we pass 8F Class 2-8-0 No 48252 on a south-bound freight near Wrexham. (4 March 1967)

Minus its smokebox number plate, BR Standard Class 5, No 73048 drifts through Shrewsbury Station in the up direction.
It has a crudely hand-painted shed code, 9K, on its smokebox door denoting that it is allocated to Bolton Motive Power Depot. The name
BOLTON is also painted in capitals on the buffer beam, a form of identification used by some locomotive depots. (4 March 1967)

BR Standard Class 5 4-6-0 No 73097 prepares to leave with a passenger train for Chester. (4 March 1967)

Just arrived with a passenger train from Chester is ex-LMS 'Black Five' 4-6-0 No 44917. It carries the smokebox shed plate bearing the legend 6A, indicating it is a Chester-based locomotive.
(4 March 1967)

In a bay platform a grimy ex-LMS 'Black Five' keeps company with a diesel multiple unit at Shrewsbury. (4 March 1967)

Just about to take water at Shrewsbury Motive Power Depot is ex-LMS 8F Class 2-8-0 No 48063.
The evocatively smoky atmosphere of a steam shed was something that warmed the heart of every enthusiast. (4 March 1967)

*Electric BoBo 'A' E3095 waits for signals at Crewe prior to departing with a parcels train. In contrast to the raucous exhaust
beats of their steam brethren, these electrics were silent and speedy as they whisked expresses between Euston, Liverpool and Manchester. (19 July 1967)*

Threading a long freight train through lines avoiding Crewe station is BR Britannia Class Pacific No 70014 'Iron Duke'. It still carried its name on the smoke deflectors, although the original metal casting had been replaced by transfers.
(19 July 1967)

An interesting trio of locomotives negotiate the complexity of track that abounds at Crewe, probably, of old, one the most well-known railway interchanges in the country. 'Black Five' No 44876 struggles with the gradient as, tender first, it drags dead diesels D285 and D1109 up the connecting line to the higher level. (19 July 1967)

Galloping down the gradient near our campsite at Garstang, 'Black Five' 4-6-0 No 44709 heads an express south towards Preston. (20 July 1967)

*Hammering through Lancaster Castle Station on a through line 9F Class 2-10-0
No 92052 snakes a long freight train southward bound. (21 July 1967)*

Ex-LMS 8F Class 2-8-0 No 48384 eases slowly through Lancaster Castle Station hauling a guards van. (21 July 1967)

About to depart with a train that will head north over the stiff climb to Shap — culminating
in grades as steep as 1 in 75 — and on towards Carlisle is 'Black Five' No 44709. (21 July 1967)

BR Standard Class 4 4-6-0 No 75015, based at Carnforth Motive Power Depot judging from its 10A shed plate, approaches Lancaster Castle Station from the north. (21 July 1967)

Carnforth was bustling with steam activity, with ex-LMS 'Black Five' 4-6-0 No 45092 shunting the sidings while sister locomotive No 44889 pulled away from the station with a freight train containing lengths of railway line. Parked in the centre was a diesel multiple unit comprising both new blue and old green liveries. In the background can be seen the tall coaling tower at Carnforth Motive Power Depot. (21 July 1967)

THE FINAL WEEK OF STEAM

CARNFORTH

As British Railways was getting rid of steam so preservationists had begun acquiring locomotives. In a siding beside Carnforth locomotive sheds was an interesting collection whose destination, fortunately, would not be the scrapyard. Here, painted in LMS 'Lake', was an ex-LMS 2MT Class 2-6-0. Formerly BR No 46441, it now carried the LMS number 6441. In its working career this locomotive never wore such gracious colours and, although smart, the livery, which would have adorned express engines, was totally unauthentic. Moving by the turntable is Sultzer diesel-electric Type 2 D5101, a class that by now, was ten years old. (28 July 1968)

Also looking forward to a happy retirement instead of the cutter's torch was ex-LMS Fairburn 4MT Class 2-6-4T No 42085.
The locomotive was sporting the early BR 'lion and wheel' emblem on its tank sides. (28 July 1968)

The biggest surprise was discovering No 61306, an example of ex-LNER B1 Class 4-6-0. Designed by Edward Thompson and introduced in 1942, it was a locomotive normally associated with the Eastern, North Eastern and Scottish Region. (28 July 1968)

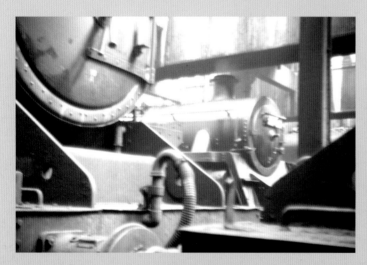

In the midst of ex-LMS 4-6-0s, the unmistakable profile of a BR Standard Class 4-6-0 could be detected in the depths of Carnforth Motive Power Depot. (28 July 1968)

The last remaining Britannia Pacific since January 1968 – No 70013 'Oliver Cromwell' – sits at the mouth of Carnforth Motive Power Depot. Now something of a celebrity, it spent the last months of its career hauling enthusiasts' specials. (28 July 1968)

A study of a 'Black Five'. Sunlight just touches the smokebox and buffer beam of No 45206 at the entrance to the locomotive shed. (28 July 1968)

Resting between two diesels outside Carnforth MPD, ex-LMS 'Black Five' 4-6-0 No 44709 is, despite the grime, a fine-looking machine. Designed by Sir William Stanier, this numerous class was first introduced in 1934 for mixed traffic. (28 July 1968)

Standard Class 9F 2-10-0 No 92091 has seen better days with its hand-painted number and 10A shed code. The 9F was the last of twelve standard designs produced by British Railways before going over to diesel traction. The last steam locomotive ever built was sister loco No 92220, 'Evening Star' in March 1960 – the only member of the class named and the only one to carry lined green livery. (28 July 1968)

Britannia Class Pacific No 70013 'Oliver Cromwell' speeds towards the camera at Bentham as it heads an enthusiasts' special from Manchester towards Carnforth via Skipton. (28 July 1968)

This page and opposite:
*BR Standard Class 4 4-6-0 locomotives Nos 75019 and 75027 were being prepared to haul an enthusiasts' special. No 75027,
under the coaling tower, was resplendent in BR Brunswick green lined out in orange and black, while No 75019, equally well turned out,
was in the more common mixed traffic livery of black lined out in red, cream and grey. (28 July 1968)*

Standard Class 4 No 75019 pilots No 75027 on the climb away from 'the other'
Clapham which is between Carnforth and Settle Junction. (28 July 1968)

'...*After a lunch of egg and tomato sandwiches and a flask of tea, I took up position on a weathered stone bridge. The sun had now penetrated the morning haze and was shining over the cornfields and meadows. In the distance I could see some of the high peaks of the mighty Yorkshire Dales. A tractor could be heard working in a field behind some trees. Occasionally, some crows would break the still of this lazy summer's afternoon with their harsh cries. The gradient was against the locomotives as they pulled away from Clapham, so I could hear their long whistle blasts and exhaust bark way before I was able to see them...*'

Diary Extract (28 July 1968)

'Black Five' super power as No 45073 pilots No 45156 'Ayrshire Yeomanry' towards Rose Grove with an enthusiasts' special. 'Ayreshire Yeomanry', along with 'Lanarkshire Yeomanry', were the only two locomotives from this numerous class to carry names. (28 July 1968)

The two Stanier 4-6-0s come to a halt by the tall home and distant signals. No 45073 and No 45156 'Ayrshire Yeomanry' then uncouple from their train and enter the motive power depot. (28 July 1968)

'Ayrshire Yeomanry' moves forward 'light engine' before reversing into the shed area. (28 July 1968)

A general view of Rose Grove MPD showing the sheds, sidings and impressive coaling tower. On the left,
superbly turned-out 8F Class 2-8-0 No 48773 backs on to the special having replaced the two 'Black Fives'. (28 July 1968)

'The signal gave the right of way and No 48773 eased its train a few yards forward. But it started slipping and stopped. The driver eased the coaches back so that, with the couplings not being taut, he could start the train without immediately taking the full strain. The engine was still a moment. People waited silently. The trail of steam and smoke rose straight in the still air. Suddenly, the wheels spun violently, the engine roared, its exhaust sounding like one long explosion – clouds of grey-black smoke billowing skywards. The blast echoed from the embankment and shed buildings. Gradually, the immaculate 8F gained control of its heavy load, its wheels now gripping the rails as it pulled up the slight gradient towards the semi-derelict station. Soon it had passed under the bridge, and out of sight, but for a long while its exhaust beats could still be heard, getting fainter and fainter as the train headed for home ...'

Diary Extract (28 July 1968)

No 48773 gets to grips with the gradient. (28 July 1968)

Creating a Vesuvian smoke display, the 8F finds its feet, making steady and vociferous progress as it gets the special underway at Rose Grove. (28 July 1968)

It's work done, No 45156 'Ayrshire Yeomanry' rests between the water tank and coaling tower. (28 July 1968)

An 8F faces the evening sun at Rose Grove in this study of a way of life just days away from being no more. (July 1968)

*Ex-LMS 8F Class 2-8-0 No 48666 is inside looking out at Rose Grove MPD
with work-weary 8F No 48493 facing the camera. (July 1968)*

I like this picture because it reminds me of an old song with lyrics that went something like: "The railway ran through the middle of the house..."
Not quite a terraced street, but the red-brick bay window might, with a stretch of the imagination, pass for someone's lounge. Clearly not a railway enthusiast's
judging by the message chalked on the window ledge: ENGINE SPOTTERS KEEP OUT! An order most enthusiasts seemed to happily ignore and one
the staff seemed reluctant to enforce. Appearing very 'neighbourly' is spruced-up 8F No 48773. (July 1968)

About to take centre stage, Stanier 8F 2-8-0 No 48773 eases past its less well-cared for class members as the heat of an August sun beats down. (July 1968)

OFF THE RAILS

'There were some rather angry railwaymen running around throwing out groups of enthusiasts. I went in the shed expecting to be thrown out myself – but I wasn't. The reason for the hot tempers was that one of the 8F Class 2-8-0s, No 48666, had disgraced itself and jumped the track near the neck of the shed. All the wheels were off except for the tender – which kept its six wheels defiantly on!

Railwaymen would come over, have a look and walk away again. There seemed to be no hurry. Meanwhile enthusiasts were taking pictures of this unfortunate iron horse looking so clumsy and helpless as it straddled the points. How it must have envied fellow class member No 48348 which was shunting trucks up and down on a piece of track across from the shed – and making full use of its last couple of days.

A pair of 8Fs coupled together, No 48340 and 48773, eased back into the shed and came out pulling breakdown trucks. They moved up to the line beside the derailed No 48666. A van then arrived with a load of men. They removed equipment from the breakdown wagons and started to jack the driving wheels of the locomotive up.

I walked out of the shed and over a road bridge to the goodsyard by Rose Grove Station, which seemed to be in a state of semi-demolition. In the yard was a 'Black Five' with a coal train. I walked along a road parallel to the railway and was now beside No 48348. From here I could look back across at the derailed engine and other locomotives in the shed.

I walked farther on to an embankment where you could look down on the main line. It sloped down to a small canal, which the railway crossed. In the distance were green fields and the National Power Station at Padiham. A signal gave the all clear and an 8F Class 2-8-0 No 48727, travelling tender first, gently eased its train of empty coal wagons across the canal, clanking past the shed area and into the yard.

I walked back past No 48348 – still shunting a few wagons...'

Diary Extract (2 August 1968)

This shot clearly shows the plight of No 48666.
All four bogie wheels and the six 6ft diameter driving wheels
are off the rails. (2 August 1968)

*Sister engines No 48340 and No 48773 haul a train of
breakdown stock out of the shed to commence the 'rescue'. (2 August 1968)*

Disaster. Ex-LMS 8F Class No 48666 has jumped the points near the neck of Rose Grove MPD.
It seemed particularly poignant this incident happened just two days before the final eclipse of steam. (2 August 1968)

Work in progress — railwaymen gather around assessing the situation. Over what seemed like a fair part of the morning, the 125-ton locomotive is jacked up under the driving wheels nearest the cab giving it an 'arched back'. Sadly, once the locomotive was rerailed, it was promptly withdrawn. (2 August 1968)

Two studies of ex-LMS 8F No 48730 at Rose Grove. This numerous class was designed by Sir William Stanier and introduced in 1935 for hauling heavy long-distance freight. (28 July 1968)

A drink at the last chance saloon? An 8F takes on water in the final days at Rose Grove MPD. By now all efforts in maintaining tidy engine roads had been given up and the area was strewn with the abandoned bric-a-brac of locomotive life. (2 August 1968)

Easing over the canal with a train of empty coal trucks is ex-LMS 8F
Class 2-8-0 No 48727 travelling tender first towards Rose Grove. (2 August 1968)

With the outline of the motive power depot, coaling tower and water tower in the background 8F No 48727 drifts past Rose Grove West Signalbox. (2 August 1968)

This page and opposite:
Busy shunting in the yard, 8F Class No 48348 is actively enjoying its last two days of liberty.
Across the tracks the breakdown train is out to re-rail 2-8-0 No 48666, which has jumped the points. (2 August 1968)

The end is near, and a tellingly forlorn atmosphere seems to hang heavy over this group of 8Fs. After the end of steam the depot lingered on for several months as a servicing point for diesels. Five years later, now derelict, it was demolished.
(28 July 1968)

The dying embers of a steam motive power depot are poignantly illustrated here as weeds and the pink spires of rose-bay-willowherbs thrive amidst neglected spaces scattered with rubble and ash. (28 July 1968)

Black locomotives, black coal and silhouettes.
This trio of 8Fs had been consigned to the condemned sidings ahead of the working remainder
of their class. Literally at the end of the line, parts of their coupling rods had been removed as
they silently awaited their fate. An 8F had a snow plough still attached to its buffer beam.
A particular irony considering we were in high summer and steam had only eight days left.

'Black Five' 4-6-0 No 44894 hurries, tender first, northwards on the West Coast Main line towards Oxenholme, the junction for the Windermere branch. Here, it passes under the B6384 between Holme and Milnthorpe. (30 July 1968)

It took a wait of about one and a half hours, and the passing of numerous diesels along this north-south mainline artery, before another steam locomotive appeared. Then unidentified 'Black Five' came hurrying along hauling its train of mixed wagons up the rising gradient of 1 in 173. (30 July 1968)

This page and opposite:
On the last Saturday of British Railways steam, what was for years an everyday scene was being acted out for the final time at Garstang and Catterall Station on the West Coast mainline between Preston and Lancaster. 'Black Five' 4-6-0 No 44806 was shunting wagons around the station sidings. Then it slowly propelled its train through the station on a loop line behind the island platform of the up side. The station closed the following year. (3 August 1968)

This page and opposite:

An evening visit to Preston Station revealed an interesting, if menial duty, for a locomotive once more at home hauling passenger and freight trains. Drifting in slowly from the south 'Black Five' No 45318 steamed through to the other end of the station. Here, it attached itself to two sleeping cars in a siding and eased them back into the station. With dusk settling and the station clock showing 8.30pm, the ex-LMS 4-6-0 seemed trapped in its own twilight zone. Relegated to steam heating duty, the 'Black Five' was warming the coaches prior to attaching them to a night service later in the evening. (31 July 1968)

FAREWELL TO BLACKPOOL STEAM

'The last steam train to Blackpool was leaving Preston at 20.48 hrs. I arrived at the station around 8.15pm and, after getting a platform ticket, it was not difficult to see which platform the train would depart from. There were masses of enthusiasts armed with cameras, tape recorders and tripods. Preston Station had been taken over by enthusiasts, and ordinary passengers looked bewildered.

Gentle music oozed from under the overall station roof canopy, only stopping when a very feminine voice informed passengers of arrival and departure times.

Just after getting to the platform, 'Black Five' No 45212 arrived from Lostock Hall MPD, passing through the station and stopping at the north end. Enthusiasts cheered. Tripods were now being set up opposite the line from which the train was due to depart, while those with flashes collected on the near platform.

About 8.25pm the Euston-Carlisle train rolled in behind a diesel. After a brief stay the Carlisle portion moved off, its passengers appearing quite entertained by the platform gathering viewed from the windows of their compartments.

The Blackpool portion remained. Here, the ordinary passengers' looks of amusement soon registered an expression more like fright as all the coaches were soon packed out to the corridors and even toilets with excited enthusiasts. But I think they began to realise they were taking part in an historic trip and began to feel a little excited themselves.

The Carlisle portion was gone and now, to roars of approval, No 45212 gently eased down to its charge. It was quite clean, with a red and white smokebox number plate and a small headboard fixed to the smokebox door: PRESTON-BLACKPOOL 3rd Aug 68 THE END OF STEAM 'FAREWELL'.

Now everyone was taking pictures. It was getting dark and flashes were going all the time. A man in a top hat and cape, along with another man, carried a violin case like a coffin and marched solemnly up and down. Everyone was excited. There was a barrage of flashes. The engine hissed loudly, and above the noise a group of people began a few bars of Auld Lang Syne. The feeling was tremendous with excitement, joy and deep sadness at this spectacle of power and sound. It was a hundred emotions all at once, as everyone was desperately trying to draw the most from those rapidly passing minutes before it was all over for ever.

At 8.50pm No 45212 gave a gruff whistle and its admirers all cheered. It eased its heavy train forward a few feet. Then the wheels skidded violently and its exhaust beats came in close succession. The roar drowned the voices of the cheering enthusiasts. Billowing smoke soared high up into the glass roof. Hot ashes shot skyward, as sparks spat from the chimney. After another burst of exhaust bark, No 45212 had controlled its train and began to ease it out of Preston Station.

Gradually, the exhaust beats came back quieter and quieter as it disappeared into the dusk with the last steam train to Blackpool. It was all over. The station was so quiet now. Enthusiasts broke up into silent bunches, hardly daring to believe that was the last of what was once an everyday sight — a steam locomotive pulling a passenger train to Blackpool.

Everyone who witnessed this event, and who had shouted and shared their emotions with fellow enthusiasts from all over Britain, had said a special goodbye to a scene that symbolised a transport world now only kept alive by memories.'

Diary Extract (3 August 1968)

Power and poignancy. Watched by a policeman, the last steam train to Blackpool departs from Preston behind a smartly turned-out 'Black Five' No 45212 complete with a red smokebox number plate and evocative headboard. (3 August 1968)

LOSTOCK HALL

Ex-LMS 8F No 48775, which had been marshalling wagons in a goods yard to the east of the station, crosses over on to the main line past Lostock Hall Station signal box. (31 July 1968)

No 48775 enters Lostock Hall Station with its mixed assortment of wagons.
(31 July 1968)

If Rose Grove housed mainly 8Fs, Lostock Hall locomotive depot was predominantly a lair of 'Black Fives'. Here is one of its most neatly turned-out residents, No 45017. (31 July 1968)

Another smart-looking 'Black Five', in steam and awaiting its next call of duty, was No 45110 resting in one of the locomotive roads outside the shed. (31 July 1968)

Lostock Hall MPD had some interesting water cranes dating back to its London and North Western Railway pre-grouping roots. Here, basking in the mid-day sun of a cloudless August day, 'Black Five' No 45110 is in the company of Stanier stablemate 8F Class 2-8-0 No 48476. (31 July 1968)

A welcome surprise lurking in the middle of the shed roads was ex-LMS Ivatt 2-6-0 Class 4MT No 43106. This class, designed for mixed traffic, had been officially extinct since the beginning of January. I understood later that this locomotive had been earmarked for preservation, and was being prepared to travel to its new home under its own steam. This class totalled 162 locomotives. They gained the nickname 'Flying Pigs' because of their front profile with a very high footplate, well clear of the cylinders. (31 July 1968)

Yet another 'Black Five' at Lostock Hall in exceedingly good external condition was No 44888. The locomotive is receiving some attention to its smokebox. (31 July 1968)

THE LAST DAY

'This was it. The last day of steam on British Railways. There would be one final fling the following Sunday, August 11, when British Railways cashed in with the famous '15 Guinea Special', but somehow that hardly seemed to count. Today was the day steam died.

In all, six steam specials were running in the North West area to mark its passing and 'Oliver Cromwell' took part in two of them.

At Blackburn No 70013 was due to arrive with its train at 14.22 but was nearly an hour late. Several times signals went up, but only to give the 'all clear' to diesels. Then, approaching the station with a special from the Accrington direction, a pair of 'Black Fives' rolled in and stopped for water.

The sun was beating down when at last the signals gave another 'all clear'. To everyone's relief 'Oliver Cromwell' came into sight piloting 'Black Five' No 44781. In honour of the occasion, No 70013 sported a set of nameplates placed over the transfer ones it had been running with on previous duties. The nameplate was red with raised letters picked out in gold. On the front of the smokebox door was a wreath.

The other special was ready to go and the 'Black Fives' started their train away from the station. Shortly after 'Oliver Cromwell' came, tender first, back through the station travelling in the same direction. It had been replaced by 8F No 48773 which had now coupled on to the front of No 44781.

The locomotives waited a while. The 8F produced a stream of black smoke, and another of white steam which rose to the sky side by side. Just ahead was the red brick entrance to Blackburn Tunnel. The signal arm swung up, and the two locomotives moved forward, their exhausts almost beating together and echoing off the walls.

Soon they were swallowed by the tunnel. Their sounds were muffled, and all we could hear was the clicking of the coach wheels as they passed over the points. As the last coach disappeared we saw it had a 'Last Day of Steam' plaque attached to its end. Now, in the silence, the signals clanked down to their original position.

Later in the afternoon at Lostock Hall the sun was glinting along the boiler of 'Oliver Cromwell'. Standing in the shed yard the locomotive looked immaculate. The sunlight was catching it at all angles as I walked along the side of it, the driving wheels nearly a foot higher than myself.

Gently simmering at Lostock Hall, on that hot Sunday afternoon of August 4, this locomotive represented the end, the last day of steam power on BR. It still seemed impossible that the reign of steam was now all but over. As I stood there two 'Black Fives' entered the shed. They had probably finished a turn on one of the six specials.

I walked around the shed. There were less steam engines than on my first visit earlier in the week. No 43106 had gone, but nothing seemed to be different inside.

Once more I went back to 'Oliver Cromwell'. There was a threatening bank of clouds coming up, but still the sun was shining down defiantly on No 70013. After a long, last look I slowly walked out of the shed. Then, as if in sympathy with the occasion, it began to rain.'

Diary Extract (4 August 1968)

An enthusiasts' special stops at Blackburn,
while double-heading 'Black Fives' No 44874 and No 45017
pause to take on water from water tanks strategically placed
at the ends of the platforms. (4 August 1968)

Running late, Britannia Pacific No 70013 'Oliver Cromwell'
pilots 'Black Five' No 44781 as the two ease their charge
towards Blackburn Station. (4 August 1968)

At the east end of Blackburn Station it is all change. 'Oliver Cromwell' has come off the train as pilot engine, and departed light engine for Lostock Hall MPD. Replacing it is 8F Class 2-8-0 No 48773, which itself has enjoyed some celebrity status on enthusiasts specials over recent weeks. (4 August 1968)

At rest at Lostock Hall MPD after having arrived 'light engine' from Blackburn, 'Oliver Cromwell' simmers quietly, soaking up the attention. There is an almost respectful air from those who have come to bid adieu to this star of the final week of steam. (4 August 1968)

AFTER THE END OF STEAM

VALE of RHEIDOL RAILWAY

THE Vale of Rheidol Railway has always been my favourite amongst the 'Great little trains of Wales'. I think this is partly because its finely proportioned 2-6-2T locomotives seemed plucky Davids to standard gauge Goliaths. Then, there is the spectacular scenery as you climb the 11 miles from Aberystwyth to Devil's Bridge, some 600ft above sea level and a world away from the seaside bustle. It is a tranquil time warp in those Cambrian Mountains where things have remained much the same down the decades. Popular attractions of the famous Mynach Falls, Jacob's Ladder and the Devil's Punchbowl have attracted visitors for generations. My first visit was on a rainy day in 1965 and I have returned a number of times since.

Having bid farewell to standard gauge steam in 1968, the diminutive Vale of Rheidol trio of 'Owain Glyndwr', 'Llywelyn' and 'Prince of Wales' became BR's final outpost of working steam, albeit in narrow gauge proportions.

They were also the only steam locomotives to carry the BR blue livery and 'Arrow' emblem. However incongruous this stamp of a modern era on vintage stock initially seemed, it offered a glimpse of what the standard gauge fleet would have looked like if, when the new livery came in, steam had not been on the way out.

The Vale of Rheidol opened in 1902. Control passed to the Cambrian Railways in 1912, which was itself absorbed by the Great Western Railway in 1923. Nationalisation came in 1948 with the Western Region running it until boundary changes put it in the charge of the London Midland Region in 1963. It remained as British Rail's only steam railway until sold to the Breckon Mountain Railway in 1989. Since then the three locomotives have sported various colour costumes harking back to past glories from their Cambrian, Great Western and British Railways days.

The Devil's Bridge terminus of the Vale of Rheidol Railway with 2-6-2T No 8, 'Llywelyn' preparing to depart for Aberystwyth with an afternoon train. The locomotive was in lined green with the late BR crest, and the coaches had V of R painted in gold on their sides. This was British Railways' only narrow gauge railway, and its only working steam locomotives after the end of standard gauge steam in 1968. (23 July 1965)

Having filled its pannier tanks with water, No 9, 'Prince of Wales', is about to collect its train which it will haul bunker-first back down the 11 dramatically-scenic miles to Aberystwyth. (September 1978)

More than a decade has passed since the previous shot and here we have a blue liveried 'Llywelyn' at Aberystwyth. No 8 prepares to run around its coaches having arrived back from Devil's Bridge and uncoupled from its train. This part of the BR station has been occupied by the narrow gauge line since 1968, the same year the V of R locomotives moved into the former BR standard gauge engine shed. Keeping brief company, and sharing the BR blue livery, is a diesel multiple unit bound for Shrewsbury. (September 1978)

A delightful journey ahead for the passengers on this train hauled by No 7 'Owain Glyndwr'. It is seen passing the former standard gauge shed – spacious headquarters for these 1ft 11 1/2ins gauge locomotives. (September 1978)

Seemingly eager to attack the gradients ahead, No 9 'Prince of Wales'
makes a rousing departure from Aberystwyth. (September 1978)

Taking water en route to Devil's Bridge at Aberffrwd is 2-6-2T No 9 'Prince of Wales'.
The oldest of the trio, No 9 was introduced in 1902, the year the line opened. (September 1978)

This image shows the low-slung shape of the locomotive and how the body spreads out from the wheelbase which runs on a 1ft 11 1/2 ins gauge track. (September 1978)

'Prince of Wales' gets ready for the stiff climb ahead as it prepares to leave Aberffrwd and head towards Devil's Bridge – a rise of 480 feet in just over four miles. (September 1978)

The exhaust of hard-working No 8 'Llywelyn' can be heard echoing off the hills as it nears the end of the line.
After this sweeping curve it enters a steep rock cutting and emerges into Devil's Bridge station. (September 1978)

'Owain Glyndwr' has arrived at Devil's Bridge. It is about to cross the points and reverse back to the water tank, which is at the entrance to the steep cutting. (September 1978)

While its passengers have strolled off from the station to savour the views, buy souvenirs at the post office or enjoy refreshments at the nearby Hafod Arms Hotel, No 9 'Prince of Wales' takes on water. (September 1978)

The fireman operates the water crane and fills the pannier tanks of No 8 'Llywelyn'. (September 1978)

With a slippery piece of track due to a recent shower, 'Llywelyn's' fireman is taking no chances. He spreads some sand on the track from a bucket for better adhesion as the locomotive prepares to ease back into the station. (September 1978)

The Vale of Rheidol's terminus at Devil's Bridge has changed very little over the decades, which is one of its enduring charms.

Full circle as, under the private ownership of the Breckon Mountain Railway, 'Owain Glyndwr' is seen evoking its BR period in lined green with the late crest and bearing a No 7 smokebox plate. We see it later, resting outside the locomotive shed at Aberystwyth.

CAMBRIAN COAST REVISITED

In 1987, during a week of glorious May weather, steam returned to the former Cambrian lines. The Cardigan Bay Express – evoking the glory days of the Cambrian Coast Express – ran twice daily between Machynlleth and Barmouth along this spectacular route of sea and mountains. The comings and goings of 'Hinton Manor' and BR Standard Class 4 4-6-0 No 75069 across the Mawddach estuary-spanning Barmouth Bridge were almost frequent enough to suggest steam had never left. For me, railway photography had come full circle. My first pictures of main line steam were taken on this route some 20-odd years previously.

It could have been the early sixties, with GWR Manor Class 4-6-0 No 7819 'Hinton Manor' easing into Machynlleth with the down Cambrian Coast Express. In fact, the Manor is running in with the empty stock of the 'Cardigan Bay Express' which travelled to Barmouth and back twice a day for a week in 1987. Duties were shared between 'Hinton Manor' and No 75069, a member of the BR Standard Class 4 4-6-0s that superseded the Manors during the last years of Cambrian steam. (May 1987)

Between two tunnels – 'Hinton Manor' approaches Penhelig Halt near Aberdovey. Having discovered this single wooden platform I was charmed by its sylvan location. Bookended between two tunnels, with the River Dovey just visible to the right and the A493 looping under it, Penhelig seemed a modeller's microcosm. (May 1987)

A perfect morning as 'Hinton Manor' hugs the coast near Llangelynnin between Towyn and Barmouth with the down Cardigan Bay Express. (May 1987)

*BR Standard Class 4 4-6-0 No 75069 embraces the gradient from Fairbourne. The locomotive, in charge
of the up Cardigan Bay Express, is seen attacking the incline towards Friog and its avalanche shelter. (May 1987)*

Dwarfed by the Cadair Idris range of mountains 'Hinton Manor', running tender first, tackles the gradient up from Fairbourne on a line that clings precariously to the cliff edge. (May 1987)

Two different days, two different locations as 'Hinton Manor' eases its train across the impressive 900 yards-long Barmouth Bridge spanning the mighty Mawddach estuary. This was a short walk from the hotel where my wife Liz and I were staying, and I remember just what stunning spring mornings these were. I also remember a chap turning up and producing secateurs to remove the ivy. I'm not a great believer in altering the flora for the sake of a shot, and also I'd intended to include it in my composition! A compromise was reached, and he left my part of the wall un-trimmed. (May 1987)

Barmouth, with its dramatic surroundings, offered many attractive photographic opportunities.
Under a rugged backcloth of mountains, 'Hinton Manor' nears its destination. (May 1987)

The weather is not always so balmy as can be seen by the small wind-blown drifts of
sand by the trackside as 'Hinton Manor' concludes its journey along the coast. (May 1987)

With a field ploughed to perfection in the foreground, and the Black Mountains in the background, BR Standard Class 4 4-6-0 No 75014 and BR Pacific No 70000 'Britannia' double-head an enthusiasts' special south at Llanvihanger, near Abergavenny en route from Hereford to Newport. The 4-6-0 is sporting the BR late crest and the Pacific has the earlier 'lion and wheel' version. (22 April 1995)

Immaculate in Southern Railway livery, King Arthur Class 4-6-0 No 828 'Sir Lamiel' eases into Salisbury Station. (9 October 1993)

With the late afternoon sun glinting along its side, BR Britannia Class Pacific No 70000 'Britannia' makes a steady departure from Salisbury. (9 October 1993)

Low gilded light enhances this view of SR 4-6-0 King Arthur Class No 828 'Sir Lamiel' as it climbs away from Sherbourne with an up special. (21 June 1992)

I was lucky enough to enjoy a brake van ride behind
ex-LSWR M7 Class 0-4-4T No 30053 which ventured
out of Salisbury Station, around the triangle of track that
made up Fisherton Tunnel Junction and Milford Junction,
and back again. Here, we are heading along the last
leg of the triangle with some healthy looking allotments
by the side of the track. (21 June 1992)

I never saw BR steam in the South Wales valleys, but I did spend an exhilarating day following the progress of BR Standard Class 4 2-6-4T No 80080 as it made several sorties up the valleys to mark the Taff Vale Railway's 150th anniversary. Here, it is seen drifting back down towards Cardiff. (October 1991)

Famous GWR steam celebrity, 'The City of Truro', puts up a sprightly performance as it speeds an enthusiasts' special along the connecting line between the Stratford-upon-Avon and Birmingham line and Hatton junction. (June 1989)

Resplendent in LNER garter blue, A4 Pacific 'Sir Nigel Gresley', makes an explosive departure from Stratford-upon-Avon.
Had Shakespeare witnessed such streamlined elegance I feel sure the Bard would have been compelled to pen a sonnet in its honour.

Ex-LNER A4 Pacific No 60009 'Union Of South Africa' arrives at Newport Station to the delight of enthusiasts and young onlookers alike.
The class of locomotive is painted on the front along with the name of the Scottish motive power depot which it resided at during the later part of its BR service.

A brief wait at a convenient footbridge at Magor was rewarded with the sight of ex-LMS Princess Royal Class Pacific 'Princess Elizabeth' pounding along this racing ground east of Newport with steam to spare as it headed out of Wales.

LMS Coronation Class Pacific No 46229 'The Duchess of Hamilton' stops at Hereford to take on water prior to departing for Newport. (October 1996)

LNER Peppercorn Class A1 Pacific No 60163 'Tornado' cuts a dash as it skirts the Teign Estuary, westward-bound, with The Torbay Express in the summer of 2009. This picturesque location was reached courtesy of permission from the owner of the right of way. Built at a cost of £3 million, 'Tornado' is the first main line locomotive constructed in the United Kingdom since 'Evening Star', the last steam locomotive built by British Railways in 1960. The original 49 A1s were all scrapped and 'Tornado', capable of 100 mph and the fastest steam loco on the UK main line, was comissioned by the A1 Steam Locomotive Trust, a charitable trust founded in 1990 to recreate an extinct class.

Making a Vesuvian exit from Plymouth is Pacific No 60163 'Tornado'. The LNER Apple Green liveried locomotive ran under its own power for the first time in July 2008 at Darlington, where it was built over a period of 14 years. It is a pleasant irony that this unique machine is newer than most modern locomotives found on today's rail network. Steam has come full circle! (8 August 2009)